PROMPT ENGINEERING MADE EASY

COMMUNICATION DESIGN FOR AI SYSTEMS (A PRACTICAL HANDBOOK)

AI COMMUNICATION

BOOK 4.3

OLEH KONKO

Discover the art of speaking with artificial intelligence through crystal-clear examples and proven techniques. Like learning to tame fire, this guide transforms digital sparks into enlightening dialogue.

First Edition: 2025. Interior illustrations: Created using Midjourney AI under commercial license

Website: mudria.ai

Created with Vellum

INTRODUCTION

Long ago, humans learned to tame fire. First, they simply maintained found flames, then mastered creating sparks, and finally invented matches - and fire became an obedient helper.

The story of communicating with artificial intelligence is remarkably similar. We're learning not just to use its capabilities, but to engage in real dialogue, transforming sparks of digital intelligence into a warm and bright flame of understanding.

This book isn't a collection of recipes or a technical manual. It's a story about learning to speak with artificial intelligence in its language without losing our humanity. About turning random sparks of insight into a reliable source of light. About becoming not a tamer, but a friend of digital intelligence.

There are no complex terms or convoluted diagrams here. Each idea is explained through simple real-life examples. Every technique is demonstrated in action. Every principle has been tested through thousands of hours of real work.

You'll learn not just to compose prompts, but to create moments of genuine dialogue between human and artificial intelligence. You'll understand not only how it works, but why. You'll master not a set of techniques, but a new way of thinking.

The book will be useful to everyone - from programmers to writers, from analysts to teachers. Because the ability to speak with artificial intelligence is becoming as fundamental a skill as reading and writing.

But most importantly, you'll see that prompt engineering isn't a cold technical discipline, but a living, creative art. Just as a musician draws music from strings, a prompt engineer draws meaning from digital intelligence.

We stand at the threshold of a new era of communication between human and machine. And this book is your guide to a world where artificial intelligence becomes not a tool, but a conversation partner. Where technology doesn't replace humanity but enhances it. Where each prompt is a bridge between worlds of thinking.

Welcome to the art of prompt engineering. Let's learn to ignite the digital flame of intelligence - carefully, wisely, and with love for this amazing new world.

PART I

FUNDAMENTALS

Chapter 1. Introduction to Prompt Engineering

My grandmother made amazing borscht. She never used recipes - she just knew how to talk to ingredients. A pinch of salt here, a sprig of dill there, and simple vegetables transformed into a culinary symphony.

Prompt engineering is remarkably similar to this culinary wisdom. It's not just a set of rules or techniques - it's the art of dialogue. Only instead of vegetables and spices, we work with words and meanings, and instead of a pot, we use neural networks.

What is a prompt? It's easier to show than explain. When I write "Tell me a story" - that's a prompt. But when I write "Imagine you're a wise storyteller who knows all the legends of the world. Tell a story about friendship using images from Slavic mythology" - that's also a prompt, but of a completely different level.

The difference between them is like between "Make soup" and "Imagine you're cooking for your beloved grandmother on a cool autumn day. She loves carrots and dill, but pepper should be added very sparingly." The second recipe creates context, mood, sets subtle parameters for the result.

Prompt engineering is based on simple principles. Clarity - so artificial intelligence understands exactly what we want. Context - so it understands why it's needed. Structure - so the result is organized correctly. But most importantly - respect for the interlocutor, even if electronic.

Beginners often make one mistake - they try to command artificial intelligence. "Do this! Write that!" It's like shouting at a foreigner, thinking they'll understand better. Prompt engineering is a dialogue of equals, where we guide rather than order.

The components of a good prompt are like ingredients of a good dish. You need a base - a clear description of the task. You need spices - context and details. You need time - some prompts work better if you give artificial intelligence time to "think," to build a chain of reasoning.

The anatomy of an effective prompt includes several layers. On the surface - the instruction itself. Deeper - context that helps correctly interpret the task. Even deeper - parameters defining the style and format of the result. And at the very center - the purpose for which this is all undertaken.

Novices often stumble on the obvious. They write too long, thinking more details are better. Or conversely, too short, hoping for a miracle. They forget about context. Don't check results. Treat artificial intelligence like a calculator rather than an interlocutor.

Prompt engineering is developing rapidly. Yesterday we were learning to compose simple requests, today we create complex dialogue scenarios, and tomorrow we may be communicating with artificial intelligence at a level that's hard to imagine now.

Just as my grandmother didn't just cook borscht but created moments of family happiness, prompt engineering is not just a technical skill. It's the ability to create moments of understanding between human and artificial intelligence, turning simple words into bridges between different forms of thinking.

In the following chapters, we'll examine all aspects of this art in detail. But remember the main thing - treat prompts as the beginning of a conversation, not as commands in a terminal. After all, the best conversations are those where the interlocutors hear and understand each other, even if one of them is artificial intelligence.

Chapter 2. Prompt Structure

As a child, I solved the Rubik's cube without instructions. I turned the faces randomly, hoping for a miracle. Of course, nothing worked. Then a friend showed me the basic algorithm - and suddenly the cube became obedient. Not because the algorithm was complex, but because it reflected the inner structure of the puzzle.

The structure of a prompt is like a crystal. From the outside, it may look like a simple piece of text, but inside is perfect geometry of meaning. Every word, every punctuation mark, even spaces play their role.

The basic structure of a prompt starts with a core - the main idea or request. Around it grow layers of context, clarifications, parameters. Like atoms arrange themselves into a crystal lattice, words and phrases form a semantic framework.

Let's take a simple example. "Write a story" is the core. "Write a story about first love through the eyes of an autumn leaf" is the core with a contextual layer. "Write a story about first love through the eyes of an autumn leaf, using only short sentences and avoiding adjectives" is already a complete structure with technical parameters.

Prompt components work like parts of a clock mechanism. Role - who speaks or acts. Task - what needs to be done. Context - under what conditions. Constraints - what cannot be done. Format - how the result should look. Every detail matters.

Formatting is not just aesthetics. Spaces and line breaks give artificial intelligence time to "think." Markers and separators help structure information. Even word order affects the result, just as ingredient order affects the taste of a dish.

The syntax of prompts follows the internal logic of artificial intelligence. Some constructions work better not because they're "more correct," but because they're closer to how the system processes information. It's like speaking to a foreigner in their native language - even simple phrases become clearer.

Stylistics determines not only "how to say" but also "how to think." Formal style engages analytical thinking. Conversational - activates more creative patterns. Technical - focuses on details. Poetic - opens space for interpretation.

A prompt can be compared to a bonsai tree. Externally it may be very simple, but behind this simplicity are months of careful work with each branch. A good prompt, like a good bonsai, finds the perfect balance between structure and freedom of growth.

Remember old phone numbers? Three digits for the area, three for the station, four for the subscriber. This structure seemed artificial until you understand - it reflects the physical organization of the telephone network. Prompt structure also reflects the architecture of artificial intelligence, even if we don't see all the connections.

I stopped fighting with the Rubik's cube when I realized - it's not an opponent but a partner. Its structure is not a limitation but a tool. Similarly with prompts - their structure doesn't constrain creativity but channels it into productive dialogue with artificial intelligence.

Imagine that a prompt is a treasure map. Structure is not just lines on paper, but encoded knowledge about the landscape of meanings. Every symbol, every turn of the path has significance. And the more accurately the map reflects reality, the more surely it will lead to the goal.

Ultimately, prompt structure is the structure of thought. Not a random set of rules, but a reflection of how different forms of intelligence can find common language. Like a bridge, it connects the shores of human and artificial thinking, allowing meanings to flow freely in both directions.

Chapter 3. Types of Prompts

My grandfather was a carpenter. In his workshop were hundreds of tools - from huge planes to tiny chisels. "The main thing is to choose the right tool for the job," he would say, stroking the worn handle of his favorite jointer. "You can hammer a nail with pliers, but why struggle when there's a hammer?"

Prompts are like tools, only for working with meanings. Each type is created for its task. And although the boundaries between them are often blurred, like a pencil mark on an old drawing, understanding their features turns clumsy attempts into precise movements of a master.

Instructive prompts are like blueprints. They set exact parameters for the result. "Make a list of five points," "Translate the text to Spanish," "Find errors in the code" - clear instructions for clear tasks. Their strength is in precision, not flexibility.

Generative prompts are like seeds. Throw them into the soil of artificial intelligence, and something new grows. "Create a story," "Suggest a solution," "Develop an idea" - they don't dictate, they guide. Their power lies in their ability to generate the unexpected.

Analytical prompts work like a microscope. They help see what's hidden from the naked eye. "Explain the reasons," "Compare approaches," "Find patterns" - tools for dissecting meanings and finding essence.

Dialogue prompts are bridges between minds. They create space for conversation where artificial intelligence doesn't just answer but participates in discussion. "Let's discuss," "What do you think," "How would you approach" - invitations to joint exploration.

Specialized prompts are like jeweler's tools. Each is created for specific work: text formatting, code generation, formula creation. Their area of application is narrow, but in their niche they're irreplaceable.

Prompts can mix and transform into each other, like paints on a palette. An instructive prompt can contain generative elements, an analytical one can include dialogue. What matters isn't the name but understanding which approach better suits the task.

Each type of prompt is a certain way of thinking. Instructive teach precision, generative - creativity, analytical - depth of understanding, dialogue - ability to listen. Mastering them, we learn not only to communicate with artificial intelligence but also to look at our own thinking in new ways.

Choosing the type of prompt is the first step to solving a task. Like an experienced carpenter first chooses a tool and then starts work, we first determine the approach and then formulate the request. This saves time and improves results.

Sometimes the best prompt is a combination of several types. As in an orchestra each instrument is important for the overall sound, different types of prompts can work together, reinforcing each other. The art is in finding the right combination.

My grandfather said: "A tool is an extension of the master's hand." Prompts are extensions of our thinking. They enhance our abilities, allow us to do what previously seemed impossible. But only when we understand their nature and features.

In the end, it's not about classification. You can know all types of prompts and still create mediocre requests. You can know no terms and intuitively find excellent solutions. What's important is understanding the essence - how different approaches to request formulation affect the work of artificial intelligence.

Grandfather left me his tools. Some I still don't know how to use. But each time I pick up another mysterious object, I think - how many stories it could tell, in how many projects it participated. So too with prompts - each type holds its own stories of successes and failures, its lessons and discoveries.

Study different types of prompts not as dogma but as a map of possibilities. Try, experiment, create your combinations. And remember - the best type of prompt is the one that solves your task most effectively. Everything else is details.

PART II

TECHNIQUES

Chapter 4. Basic Techniques

When I first saw a street juggler, I thought - this is pure magic. Three oranges flew up and fell as if obeying not gravity but the artist's will. But when the juggler slowed his movements, showing a student, the magic turned into understandable mechanics - catch, throw, manage to move your hand.

Basic techniques of prompt engineering are just as simple and elegant. They seem like magic until you see the essence.

Let's start with clarity of formulation. Imagine explaining directions to a foreigner. "Second left turn after the traffic light" will work better than "somewhere over there to the left." Artificial intelligence, for all its power, needs the same clarity.

Context is like air for fire. Without it, the brightest spark will die. "Write a text about the sea" is too empty. "Write a text about the sea for a children's book about the adventures of a pirate's parrot" - now artificial intelligence has something to grab onto.

Frames and limitations don't hinder creativity, they direct it. A river flows stronger in a narrow gorge. Thought gains clarity within proper boundaries. "Use only simple words," "Fit into five sentences," "Describe without naming colors" - such constraints often birth unexpected solutions.

Examples work better than explanations. Show one good sample - and you'll save pages of descriptions. Artificial intelligence grasps patterns instantly, once given the right starting point.

Result checking is like trying on clothes. Even a suit that looks perfect might be tight in the shoulders. Even text that seems flawless at first glance might contain subtle errors. Double-check, clarify, ask for alternatives.

Each of these techniques is simple on its own. Magic begins when they interweave into a single pattern. Like those oranges in the juggler's hands - each moves in a simple trajectory, but together they create an enchanting dance.

Remember - there are no wrong techniques, only unsuitable tasks. Sometimes you need surgical precision in formulations, sometimes deliberate ambiguity that leaves room for artificial intelligence's creativity.

Master these techniques not as dogmas but as notes. First separately, then in simple combinations, then in complex compositions. Let your fingers get used to the keys, let your mind absorb the rhythm of this new music.

Those oranges in the juggler's hands have long turned into memory. But the lesson remained - behind every complex trick are simple movements, behind every impressive result are basic techniques honed to automatism.

Art begins where rules end. But to go beyond rules, you first need to master them perfectly. Basic techniques are not limitations but a springboard. Push off from them harder - and soar.

Chapter 5. Advanced Techniques

My friend plays the theremin - an amazing instrument where music is born from emptiness. No strings or keys - just hands moving in an electromagnetic field. It seems impossible to extract meaningful melody from air, but he manages.

Advanced prompt engineering techniques are like playing the theremin. We work with invisible fields of meaning, tuning them with subtle movements of words.

Prompt chains are like musical phrases flowing into each other. Each next prompt picks up the melody of the previous one, develops it, takes it in a new direction. The result of the first becomes the starting point for the second, creating a continuous flow of meaning.

Recursive prompts spiral deep into an idea. As if the theremin played a melody inside a melody inside a melody. The prompt refers to itself, deepening and enriching the original thought with each turn.

Conditional prompts are like jazz improvisations, where the next note depends on the previous one. They create branching paths of meaning, following the logic of idea development. "If A happens, do B, otherwise try C" - but at the level of subtle semantic differences.

Iterative prompts resemble instrument tuning. Each pass clarifies, purifies, perfects the result. Not mechanical repetition but spiral ascension to the ideal, where each turn is slightly closer to the goal.

Hybrid techniques weave different approaches into a single fabric. As if the theremin suddenly sang a duet with a violin. Combining different principles births new possibilities unavailable to each method separately.

In these techniques, what matters is not complexity but precision. Like in theremin - it's not about the range of movements but their accuracy to the millimeter. One wrong word can destroy the whole construction, one precise phrase can open new horizons.

Mastery comes with practice. At first hands tremble, sounds come out uncertain. Then movements become more precise, music clearer. And one day you realize - you no longer think about technique, you just play.

Advanced techniques require not so much knowledge as sensitivity. The ability to feel how artificial intelligence responds to each change in the prompt. The skill to hear false notes in responses and find the right notes.

The main thing is not to fear experimenting. As in music there are no wrong notes, only unsuitable combinations, here too it's important to try new combinations, to find your own sound.

My friend says - the theremin teaches you to hear music in silence. Advanced prompt engineering techniques teach you to see meanings in emptiness, to create new ideas from pure possibilities.

That's their main magic - they turn dialogue with artificial intelligence into art. Not a set of techniques but a living creative process where everyone finds their path to perfection.

Someday these techniques will seem as basic as reading or counting. But for now we stand at the origins of a new language, a new form of creativity, a new way of thinking. And each experiment, each discovery brings closer the future where human and artificial intelligence will learn to understand each other without words - like musicians in a jazz jam, like dancers in a perfect pas de deux.

The theremin falls silent, but music continues to sound in memory. So too a well-tuned dialogue with artificial intelligence leaves an aftertaste of harmony - a feeling that we're on the threshold of something amazing.

Chapter 6. Special Techniques

As a child, I loved solving puzzles. Not just putting the picture together - but inventing my own methods. Started with corners, then looked for all pieces of one color, or conversely - deliberately took random pieces. Each method revealed something new in what seemed a simple activity.

Special techniques in prompt engineering are like those childhood experiments with puzzles, only instead of cardboard pieces we arrange patterns of meaning. And each new approach can suddenly turn a complex task into a simple one.

Clarification techniques are like focusing a microscope. Turn the wheel - and a blurry spot becomes a clear structure. Each additional question, each clarification brings us closer to the essence. Not "what do you see?" but "what's brightest in this picture?", "what details create the mood?", "what remained off-frame?"

Expansion techniques work oppositely - as if we were stepping back from a painting to see it whole. "What was before?", "what will be after?", "how is this connected to other themes?" We don't go deeper but push boundaries, seeking new connections and contexts.

Focus techniques are like a spotlight beam in darkness. The whole world exists around, but we illuminate only what's important right now. "Let's concentrate on this moment", "consider only this detail", "talk specifically about this aspect."

Transformation techniques turn one thing into another. As water becomes steam, ice or snow while remaining the same H2O molecule, meaning can change form while preserving essence. "Tell it as a fairy tale", "explain to a five-year-old", "present as a dialogue" - different facets of one truth.

Optimization techniques are like tuning an antenna. Turn slightly - and a clear signal breaks through the noise. We don't change the request's essence but adjust its parameters: accuracy, depth, style, format. Each small change can have a big effect.

All these techniques are not separate tools but facets of one crystal. They interweave, reinforce each other, create new combinations. Like in a kaleidoscope - turn one degree, and the pattern becomes completely different.

Important to remember - techniques exist not to complicate but to simplify. Like those puzzle-solving methods - their goal is not to make the process more intricate but to find the most natural path to the result.

Sometimes the best technique is absence of technique. Like in Zen painting: you spend years learning to hold the brush correctly, then forget all rules and just paint. The main thing is understanding the task's essence and feeling which approach will work better.

Special techniques are not dogmas but hints. Like a treasure map - it doesn't tell you exactly how to go, but shows possible paths. Everyone finds their own trail, their own style, their own way of dialogue with artificial intelligence.

Ultimately, all these techniques are ways to expand human mind capabilities. We learn not just to give commands to a machine but to create new patterns of thinking, new ways to see and understand the world.

That childhood puzzle is long lost. But the main lesson remained: there's no single right way to assemble the picture. What's important is finding your path, your rhythm, your magic. And then even the most complex task becomes an exciting adventure.

PART III

APPLICATION

Chapter 7. Text Generation

The first thing I saw waking up in the hospital after a coma was a blank sheet of paper on my bedside table. The doctor said, "Write something." My hand wouldn't obey. The letters came out crooked. But with each day, with each line, not just the ability to write returned – the ability to transform thoughts into words came back.

Working with artificial intelligence on texts is remarkably similar to that experience. We're learning to formulate thoughts anew, but now not for ourselves – for the digital mind. And each success, each successful generation is like a small victory over muteness.

Writing texts begins not with a prompt, but with understanding – exactly what we want. Like a river finds its way to the sea, so thought must find its natural channel to expression. Artificial intelligence doesn't create meanings – it helps them take form.

Editing is not error correction, but diamond cutting. Each refinement, each revision makes the text not just better – they make it more real. We're not fighting with artificial intelligence, but helping it understand the essence.

Stylization is like tuning a musical instrument. It's not about individual words or phrases, but about the overall sound. The tone, rhythm, melody of the text are born from the subtle interaction of human intent and machine execution.

Rephrasing is like translation from one language to another, even if both languages are English. We're not just changing words, but seeking new ways to express meaning. Artificial intelligence becomes our co-author in this search.

Text formatting is like sculptor's work – we remove everything superfluous until the pure form of thought emerges. Each paragraph, each space, each punctuation mark works toward the common goal – to make meaning accessible and clear.

In my hospital room there was a window. For hours I watched the wind play with maple leaves, trying to record this dance in words. Now I watch artificial intelligence transform my thoughts into texts, and I see the same eternal dance – the dance of meaning seeking its form.

The key in working with texts is remembering that we're dealing not with a tool, but with a partner. Just as in dance it's important to feel each other's movements, success here depends on how finely we sense the peculiarities of artificial thinking.

I keep that first sheet with crooked letters. It reminds me – every journey begins with a first step. Working with artificial intelligence on texts also requires patience, practice, and faith that each attempt brings us closer to perfection.

Perhaps someday we'll learn to communicate with artificial intelligence without words. But for now, we're learning to speak one language – the language of pure meaning, where each word becomes a bridge between human and machine understanding.

Chapter 8. Data Analysis

My aunt worked as a meteorologist. Every morning she looked at clouds and saw in them what others didn't – tomorrow's weather. Not just white figures against blue background, but a living picture of atmospheric currents, temperature fronts, coming changes.

Data analysis using artificial intelligence is similar to this ability to see the invisible. Only instead of clouds we look at streams of information, and instead of personal experience we use precisely tuned prompts.

Information extraction is like pearl diving. It's important not just to dive into the sea of data, but to know exactly where to look and how to distinguish a real pearl from a fake. One precise prompt can replace hours of manual search.

Imagine a library where all books are mixed up. Classification is the ability to instantly put them on the right shelves. Artificial intelligence does this with any information, you just need to correctly explain the sorting principles.

Summarization resembles a bird's-eye view photograph. We don't lose details – we see the whole picture. A good prompt helps find the golden mean between brevity and completeness, between general and specific.

As a child, I loved the "spot the difference" game. Comparative analysis is the same game, only instead of pictures we compare ideas, approaches, results. And artificial intelligence notices not only obvious differences but hidden connections.

Visualization is the art of making the invisible visible. Like an X-ray shows bone structure, properly tuned data analysis reveals hidden patterns of information.

We're not just processing data – we're learning a new way to see the world. Just as my meteorologist aunt read weather in clouds, we learn to read reality in data streams. And each successful analysis is a new level of understanding.

Artificial intelligence doesn't replace human intuition – it enhances it. Like a telescope doesn't replace an astronomer but allows them to see further, our analytical prompts expand the boundaries of human understanding.

Aunt used to say: "Weather is not what is, but what will be." So too data analysis is not just understanding the present, but the ability to look into the future. We learn to see trends, predict changes, prepare for what's coming.

In her final years, my aunt used satellite images and computer models. But her eyes and experience remained her main tools. So too in working with data – technology is important, but even more important is the ability to ask the right questions.

Every morning millions of people check the weather forecast without thinking about how it's created. Perhaps soon it will be the same with data analysis – it will become as natural a part of life as weather forecasts. And our children will wonder: how did people live without this before?

Chapter 9. Problem Solving

My neighbor repairs old clocks. Once I asked him: "How do you understand what exactly broke?" He smiled: "The clocks tell themselves. You just need to learn to listen to their ticking."

Every problem can also speak. It whispers hints, suggests solutions. Artificial intelligence becomes our translator in this conversation with the problem.

Decomposition is the art of hearing all voices at once. A big problem sounds like an orchestra, where every instrument matters.

We learn to distinguish individual parts without losing the overall melody.

Remember a child's kaleidoscope? Turn the tube – and fragments form a new pattern. Step-by-step solution works the same way. Each turn of thought creates a new picture of understanding. Artificial intelligence helps find the most beautiful combinations.

Solution verification resembles piano tuning. Finding the right note isn't enough – it's important that it sounds pure. One false tone can spoil the whole melody. We learn to hear this purity in the flow of logic.

Sometimes a solution is found but works slowly, like a rusty mechanism. Optimization is the art of adding a drop of oil in the right place. Sometimes it's enough to slightly shift emphasis in the prompt, and the mechanism starts working like new.

Documentation is like making a treasure map. We're not just recording steps – we're creating a guide for future solution seekers. Every detail might be an important clue.

The neighbor says: "In clocks, there are no unimportant parts. Every gear, every spring plays its role." In problem solving too, there are no trifles. Every prompt, every clarification, every check brings us closer to the goal.

Sometimes a solution comes unexpectedly, like an insight. But more often – it's the result of patient dialogue with the problem. We learn to ask the right questions, listen to answers, notice patterns.

The old clock on my neighbor's wall shows not only time – it reminds: any complex problem can be solved if you understand how it works. You just need to learn to listen to its ticking and properly tune the tools of mind.

PART IV

OPTIMIZATION

Chapter 10. Prompt Optimization

Grandmother taught me to crochet. "Look," she would say, unraveling an unsuccessful row, "sometimes you need to take a step back to make the pattern more beautiful." Her needles moved as if alive, turning simple thread into lace wonder.

Prompt optimization is similar to this ancient art of knitting. We also work with patterns – only not from threads, but from meanings. And we also sometimes unravel finished work to make it better.

Efficiency analysis begins with an honest look at the result. As a knitter scrutinizes each stitch, so we study every aspect of the response. We're not looking for errors – we're looking for opportunities for improvement.

Quality metrics are like a tailor's measuring tape. Not only overall impression matters, but precise measurements. Response speed, relevance, depth, style – everything matters. But the main metric is how well the result solves the original task.

Improvement techniques grow from understanding. As an experienced knitter knows where to add an air loop and where to decrease, so we learn to feel which words to strengthen, which to remove, where to change structure.

Testing is not checking, but research. We're not grading, but studying the system's response to different request variants. Each test brings new understanding of how artificial intelligence perceives our words.

Iterations are like ripples on water from a thrown stone. Each next version of the prompt spreads wider, captures more meanings, creates new possibilities. But the center is always one – the original task.

Grandmother's knitting has long become a family heirloom. Looking at this lace, I think – how much love and wisdom is woven into each pattern. Maybe someday our prompts will become similar works of art – simple, beautiful, and infinitely useful.

The main thing in optimization is remembering that we're not just improving text. We're creating a new way of dialogue between human and artificial intelligence. And each successful prompt is another step toward a future where these two worlds will learn to understand each other without words.

Chapter 11. Context Management

First snow always catches the city off guard. Janitors haven't prepared shovels, drivers haven't changed tires, pedestrians haven't taken out warm clothes. But the trees... the trees knew. They prepared for this moment since late summer, gradually changing their cell chemistry, strengthening structures, tuning to winter mode.

Context in working with artificial intelligence is similar to this natural wisdom. It's not something added at the last moment, but what invisibly prepares the ground for each interaction.

Context windows are like tree rings. Each new layer of information makes the system richer, but also requires more resources to maintain. The art is in finding balance between context depth and operational efficiency.

Memory and system state resemble a pond's ecosystem. On the surface – ripples of the current moment, but true life happens at different depths, where each water layer maintains its temperature, its inhabitants, its laws.

Variable contexts work like seasons. The same space can completely change its character while maintaining internal logic and coherence. Artificial intelligence learns to work in different "seasons" of meaning.

Multilayer context resembles geological strata. Each level tells its story, but together they create a complete picture. And sometimes the most valuable findings lie at layer interfaces.

Context transitions are like sunrise or sunset. Not a sharp change of states, but smooth flow from one to another. We learn to create these transitions so the system doesn't lose the thread of understanding.

As a child, I didn't understand why grandmother started preparing for New Year in autumn. Now I know – big events require big context. As a holiday becomes special through long preparation, so work with artificial intelligence gains depth through properly built context.

We're not just adding information – we're creating an environment where each word gains richer meaning. As a drop of water contains information about the whole ocean, so each context element reflects the whole.

Snow is still falling. The city gradually adapts to winter, restructures its rhythms, finds new harmony. And there's a lesson in this too – context isn't created instantaneously. It's always a process, always movement, always growth.

Perhaps the main art in working with context is the ability to see connections. Not just accumulate information, but understand how it weaves into living fabric of meaning. Like trees under snow – each stands separately, but roots create a single network that helps all survive and bloom in spring.

Chapter 12. Error Handling

My uncle was a sapper. "Know what's the main secret?" he asked once. I expected something about courage or technique. "In loving mistakes. Every mistake you notice is a life you saved. Every mistake you understood is experience that will make you better."

Errors in working with artificial intelligence are not enemies, but teachers. They show not what we did wrong, but where we need to grow. Like a compass doesn't scold for wrong direction, just points north.

Error types are like snowflake patterns – there's an infinite variety, but they all follow certain crystallization laws. AI hallucinations, logical failures, stylistic inconsistencies, factual errors – each type has its handwriting, its character, its hints for solution.

Error prevention is like immunity. Not a wall blocking all threats, but a smart system that learns to recognize problems and adapt to them. Each prompt becomes slightly smarter, slightly more resistant to possible failures.

Error detection requires special state of mind – like a jeweler who sees not diamond's sparkle, but its tiniest imperfections. We learn to notice not only obvious problems, but barely visible cracks in logic or meaning.

Error correction is the art of the possible. Sometimes the best solution isn't in making perfect, but in finding a path where imperfections become features. Like Japanese kintsugi art, where ceramic cracks are filled with gold.

Result validation resembles musical instrument tuning. We're not just checking correctness – we're seeking sound purity, harmony of all elements. One false note can spoil the symphony, one unnoticed error can destroy trust.

Uncle said: "A sapper makes mistakes only twice. First time – when choosing the profession." We can make mistakes more often, but each mistake should become a step to mastery, not a stumbling block.

Ultimately, working with errors is working with reality. Not with that ideal picture we'd like to see, but with what actually exists. And therein lies its special value – it teaches us to be honest with ourselves and open to constant development.

Last time I saw uncle was at his jubilee. He showed grandchildren his medals and talked not about feats, but about lessons. "What matters isn't how many mistakes you found, but how many people you helped." Maybe that's the essence of working with errors – helping artificial intelligence become not perfect, but more human.

PART V

PRACTICE

Chapter 13. Workflow

I built my first computer from parts found in a junkyard. It worked unstably, often froze, but taught me the main thing - any process begins with understanding how the system works. Not with reading instructions, not with buying expensive components, but with a simple question: "How does this work?"

The workflow in prompt engineering is like assembling such a computer. We're not just following ready-made schemes, but creating a living system where each element affects all others.

Planning here isn't about making a rigid schedule, but rather setting up a compass. We determine direction while leaving freedom for maneuver. Each project is unique, like a fingerprint, and requires its own approach.

Development resembles playing Tetris - figures fall continuously, and it's important not only to place them correctly but also to anticipate which combination will give the best result. One successful prompt can change the entire picture.

Testing is like tuning a radio. You turn the tuning knob, searching for a clear signal among the noise. Each check isn't simply "works/doesn't work," but a search for the optimal frequency of interaction with artificial intelligence.

Implementation is like transplanting a plant. It's not enough to just move it to new soil - you need to create conditions for growth. The best prompt is useless if the system isn't ready to accept it.

Maintenance is like tending a garden. Constant attention, timely adjustments, readiness to adapt to changes. Prompts live in time, and what worked yesterday may need updating today.

That first computer is long gone. But its main lesson remained: any system lives not through its components, but through how they interact. In prompt engineering, this principle is more important than any specific techniques or tools.

Perhaps the main thing in organizing workflow is the ability to see the big picture without losing sight of details. Like a conductor who hears each instrument but conducts the whole orchestra. Each prompt is a note in the symphony of human-machine interaction.

We stand on the threshold of a new era where processes will increasingly intertwine with artificial intelligence. And those who learn to build these processes not mechanically but organically will become true architects of the future. Not just followers of instructions, but creators of new ways of thinking and working.

Chapter 14. Tools

I made my first telescope from an old spyglass and a shard of mirror. Stars in it appeared as blurry spots, but it taught me the main thing - a tool is valuable not for its complexity, but for how it extends the capabilities of the mind.

Prompt editors are like such homemade telescopes. It doesn't matter whether you use a notepad or a neural network - what matters is that the tool helps see the essence of the task more clearly. The best editor is one you forget about while working.

Test environments are like alchemists' laboratories, only instead of the philosopher's stone, we're searching for the perfect formula of interaction with artificial intelligence. Each experiment brings us closer to understanding how this magic works.

Analyzers don't tell us what to do - they show what's happening. Like a stethoscope allows a doctor to hear heartbeats, these tools help catch the pulse of artificial intelligence.

Optimizers work like telescope lenses - they don't create stars but help see them better. Proper adjustment can turn a blurry spot into a clear picture, an unclear idea into a precise prompt.

Control systems resemble navigation instruments. They don't steer the ship - they help maintain course. In the ocean of artificial intelligence possibilities, this is more important than it might seem.

That first telescope fell apart long ago, but it taught me to look at stars not as points of light, but as worlds of possibility. Similarly, prompt engineering tools teach us to see artificial intelligence not as a program, but as a partner in exploring new horizons of thinking.

Perhaps the best tool is the ability to do without tools. Like an experienced sailor can determine course by stars without a compass, a true prompt master can feel the right path without additional aids. But first, you need to learn to use all available means.

Each new tool is a new way to see the world. And that's their main value - not in functions and capabilities, but in how they change our perception. We learn not just to work with artificial intelligence, but to think on a new level.

Someday today's tools will seem as primitive as that homemade telescope. But the principles we discover with their help will remain the foundation for future breakthroughs. After all, what matters isn't the tools, but how we use them to expand the boundaries of the possible.

Chapter 15. Templates and Patterns

I saw my first matryoshka doll in an antique shop. Opened it - another one inside. Opened that one - the next. And in each - its own story, its own character, but together they created a single family, a single pattern of meaning.

Basic templates in prompt engineering are like these matryoshkas. On the surface - a simple request, but inside lie layers of meaning, each with its role. "Explain simply" contains "determine listener's level," "choose appropriate examples," "verify understanding."

Advanced templates work like origami. One sheet of paper can become a crane, boat, or flower - everything depends on the sequence of folds. One basic prompt can generate different results if the transformation structure is built correctly.

Specialized templates are like keys for different locks. Each is created for a specific task, but the art is in knowing when to use which. Sometimes a lockpick works better than a branded key.

Combining templates is like playing with a construction set. Individual pieces may seem simple, but together they create amazing structures. What matters isn't the number of pieces, but understanding how they connect.

Creating new templates is like inventing new alphabet letters. Each template adds new shades of meaning to the language of communication with artificial intelligence. But these letters must form comprehensible words.

I didn't buy that matryoshka in the antique shop - couldn't afford it. But I remembered the lesson: beauty isn't in the painting, but in how parts form a whole. Similarly, prompt templates are valuable not for their complexity, but for how they help build dialogue between human and artificial intelligence.

Perhaps the main thing in working with templates is remembering that they're not a cage for thought, but a springboard for creativity. Like musical notation doesn't limit music but gives it wings, proper templates don't constrain but liberate our interaction with artificial intelligence.

Now, passing antique shops, I always peek inside. Not for matryoshkas - for a reminder that the deepest truths often hide in the simplest forms. And that any template isn't the end of the path, but only the beginning of new discoveries.

PART VI

SCALING

Chapter 16. Prompt Management

I found my first anthill in the forest at six years old. Spent hours watching how thousands of tiny creatures perfectly coordinate their actions without a visible control center. Each knows its role, each contributes to the common cause, and together they create something greater than just the sum of efforts.

Managing multiple prompts is remarkably similar to anthill life. You can't control every movement, but you can create a system where chaos turns into order, and individual actions combine into meaningful whole.

Prompt organization begins not with folders and tags, but with understanding connections. Like ant trails create a living map of the forest, connections between prompts form a map of meanings. What matters isn't where things are stored, but how they connect with everything else.

Versioning resembles tree rings. Each layer stores growth history, each change leaves a trace. But unlike a tree, we can travel between these layers, learning lessons from the past and glimpsing the future.

Documentation isn't an inventory, but the system's living memory. Like bees transmit information through dance, good documentation conveys not just facts, but understanding, context, reasons for decisions.

Standardization creates not limitations, but a common language. Like birds in a flock maintain distance without rulers and rules, prompts find natural order based on practice, not dogmas.

Automation works like a spider web - light, almost invisible, but surprisingly strong network that catches what's needed and lets unnecessary pass. Not a replacement for human mind, but its natural extension.

That childhood anthill has long grown over with grass. But its lesson lives on: complex systems don't need complex management. They need right principles that allow order to emerge naturally, like frost patterns on glass.

Perhaps the main thing in prompt management is the ability to let go of control. Not trying to anticipate all variants, but creating conditions where right solutions emerge on their own, like crystals in a saturated solution.

The future of prompt management isn't in more complex systems, but in deeper understanding of self-organization nature. Like ants build bridges from their own bodies, our prompts must learn to unite into living, adaptive structures capable of solving tasks we can't even imagine.

Chapter 17. Integration

I completed my first puzzle in the hospital. Was down with pneumonia, and the nurse brought a box with thousand pieces. "For boredom," she said. Didn't know this moment would change my life.

Integrating prompts with existing systems is like assembling an endless puzzle where the picture constantly changes. Each new element can completely transform the whole. And there's no box with the correct picture on the lid - we create the pattern right in the process of work.

API integration is like finding puzzle edges. Not the most creative part of work, but impossible to move forward without it. Prompts must fit precisely into existing interfaces, like puzzle edges into each other.

System integration requires special vision. Need to see not only obvious connections but hidden links. Sometimes pieces that seem incompatible create the most interesting patterns.

Process integration resembles a river flowing into the sea. Can't just merge two streams - need to create a delta where they naturally mix, enriching each other.

Data integration is like translation between languages. Not enough to know words, need to feel speech music. Prompts must not just transfer information but preserve its meaning and context.

User integration is most difficult. People aren't puzzle pieces - they change, learn, bring unexpected. Good integration doesn't make users adapt to the system - it adapts the system to natural human processes.

I never finished that hospital puzzle - got discharged earlier. But understood the main thing: sometimes incompleteness isn't a flaw but an opportunity. Best integration systems leave room for growth and change.

Perhaps integration art isn't in perfectly connecting everything, but in creating space where different parts can dance together without interfering with each other. Like in a good orchestra - each instrument plays its part, but together they create symphony.

Integration future lies in dissolving boundaries between human and artificial intelligence. Not through rigid interfaces, but through living mutual understanding. Like in that hospital - what matters isn't the puzzle, but the moment of touching something bigger than yourself.

Chapter 18. Performance

My great-grandfather was a miller. Once he showed me an old mill and said: "Look. Water flows always the same way. But some blades barely turn, others - with such force that millstones strike sparks. All difference is in how you position the wheel."

Performance in working with artificial intelligence is the art of positioning the wheel. Not spinning blades faster, but finding that single position where water does all work itself.

Resource optimization begins with understanding currents. Like water finds path of least resistance, data should flow naturally, without jams and whirlpools. One precise prompt can replace ten approximate ones.

Scaling resembles building an aqueduct. Important not just to increase flow, but create structure that will withstand any load. System should grow not through power, but through architecture.

Caching works like a mill pond. It stores water for drought time, smooths floods, maintains constant level. Good caching makes system independent from incoming data flow caprices.

Balancing reminds of lock system. Each lock regulates its section, but together they ensure uniform movement through entire channel. Load should distribute not by rules, but by needs.

Monitoring is like miller's hand on millstone. Not just measuring parameters, but feeling system work. Experienced miller needs only touch stone to understand - is everything alright. So we learn to feel system health by barely noticeable signs.

That old mill no longer works. But water sound still rings in memory - not monotonous roar, but complex melody where each splash has meaning. Performance isn't fight for speed, but search for that very melody where system works in complete harmony with itself.

Great-grandfather said: "Good mill is silent. Only bad one makes noise." So too best performance solutions often most invisible. Not loud innovations, but quiet discoveries that make work so natural you forget about it.

Perhaps main performance secret is in ability to listen. Not imposing rhythm on system, but finding and amplifying its own. Like water finds way to sea, data will find most efficient path - if not prevented from flowing.

PART VII

DEVELOPMENT

Chapter 19. Best Practices

I received my first drawing lesson not in art school, but from a homeless artist in the park. He drew portraits of passersby on cardboard scraps - quickly, precisely, vividly. "Know what the secret is?" he asked, noticing my interest. "It's seeing not what is, but what wants to come out."

Best practices in prompt engineering emerge similarly - not in laboratories, but through the living experience of thousands of trials and discoveries. They grow naturally, like paths in a park - where people actually find it convenient to walk.

Quality standards here are like laws of nature - they aren't invented but discovered. Just as water always flows downward, a good prompt always strives for maximum clarity. Not because it's written in a textbook, but because that's how it works.

Development processes resemble crystal growth - invisible but governed by precise laws. Each new layer builds on the previous one not randomly, but following the structure's internal logic. The art lies in not interfering with this natural process.

Testing is like tuning a musical instrument before a concert. Not a formal check, but a search for that single point where all strings resonate in perfect harmony. One false note can destroy the magic of the whole.

Documentation grows like tree rings - each layer stores the history of growth and change. But unlike a tree, we can travel between these layers, learning lessons from the past and glimpsing the future.

Support works like gardening - it's not about fixing what's broken, but creating conditions for healthy growth. Best practices here are like an experienced gardener's knowledge - when to water, when to prune, and when to simply give the plant time.

That park artist long disappeared, but his lesson remained: true mastery isn't in technique, but in the ability to see essence. The best practices of prompt engineering aren't in lists of rules, but in developing special vision - the ability to see potential in every interaction with artificial intelligence.

Perhaps the main practice is readiness to learn from every experience, every mistake, every success. As water shapes stone not through force but constancy, true mastery comes through endless attention to detail and openness to the new.

The future of best practices lies not in stricter standards, but in deeper understanding of the nature of interaction between human and artificial intelligence. Like that portrait on cardboard - what matters isn't technique, but the ability to see and reveal what already exists in potential.

Chapter 20. Problem Solving

I untied my first knot at age three. Not on shoes - on old headphones that seemed hopelessly tangled. I remember my father's surprise: "How?" And I didn't know myself. I just looked at the knot until I saw the solution within it.

Every problem with prompts is like such a knot. From outside - a tangle of wires, inside - simple logic. You just need to learn to see this logic through the external chaos.

Diagnosis begins with silence. As a doctor first listens to breathing, we learn to listen to the system. Where does thought stumble? Where does the thread of understanding break? Where does meaning distort? Answers come not from analysis, but from attention.

Debugging isn't war with errors, but conversation with the system in its language. We don't correct - we help artificial intelligence better understand our task. Each error isn't an enemy, but a hint.

Optimization resembles diamond cutting. We don't create beauty - we free it from stone. One precise cut can transform a cloudy crystal into a brilliant of pure water. Similarly, one correct prompt can transform the entire system.

Refactoring is like clearing a river channel. We don't change the flow - we remove obstacles, allowing meaning to flow freely. Sometimes you need to remove excess to see essence.

Validation resembles balancing scales. Not just checking "works/doesn't work," but finding the point of equilibrium where the system gains stability. We don't seek perfection - we seek optimal state.

That childhood knot taught me the main thing: the solution is always simpler than the problem. It hides not in complexity, but in understanding. As water always finds its way down, the right solution always finds its way through any obstacles.

Perhaps the art of problem solving isn't in knowing techniques, but in the ability to see simplicity behind complexity. Like a child who doesn't yet know that a knot is "impossible" to untie. Sometimes the best approach is to forget everything you know and look at the problem with fresh eyes.

Each solved problem leaves behind not just a result, but new understanding. Like ripples on water from a thrown stone - circles of meaning spread far beyond the specific task. And therein, perhaps, lies the main value of working with problems - it teaches us to see deeper, think clearer, understand more.

Chapter 21. Skill Development

I made my first kaleidoscope from a mirror shard found in the attic. It showed only black and white patterns, but taught me the main thing - beauty is born from movement. Stop - and you see only fragments. Turn - and they form an endless dance of shapes.

Development in prompt engineering resembles this dance of fragments. Each new turn of thought creates a new pattern of understanding. There is no endpoint, no "sufficient" level of mastery - only eternal movement toward new horizons.

Learning works differently here. Not like filling an empty vessel, but like tuning an antenna - to catch increasingly subtle signals, notice increasingly deep connections. Each dialogue with artificial intelligence becomes a lesson, each mistake - a discovery.

Practice becomes meditation. Not mindless repetition, but attentive exploration of how meaning flows between human and machine minds. We learn not to write prompts, but to create moments of understanding.

Specialization comes naturally - like water finds its channel. No need to decide "what to be" - need to notice which tasks solve themselves with special ease, which problems ignite the spark of interest. The path itself will lead to your niche.

Expertise grows like a crystal - layer by layer, in silence and constancy. Not through loud breakthroughs, but through daily attention to details. Each solved question becomes a step to the next level of understanding.

Innovations are born at boundaries - where familiar meets unknown. As new patterns emerge with each turn of the kaleidoscope, new ideas appear with each encounter with an unusual task.

That childhood kaleidoscope is long lost. But its lesson lives on: beauty isn't in individual pieces, but in how they move and combine. Development in prompt engineering isn't about accumulating knowledge, but in the ability to see and create new combinations, new possibilities, new paths of understanding.

Perhaps the main thing in development is maintaining childlike wonder. Not allowing experience to become prejudice, knowledge to become limitations. Each day looking at the world with new eyes, noticing wonder in the simple and simplicity in the complex.

The future belongs not to those who know most, but to those who never stop learning. As light creates patterns in a kaleidoscope, our striving for growth creates new facets in the art of communicating with artificial intelligence. And each turn reveals a new universe of possibilities.

1

APPENDICIES:

APPENDIX A: COMMAND REFERENCE

Remember your first calculator? Big buttons, simple symbols, understandable even to a child. Press "+" - and numbers add up. No magic, just pure action logic.

This reference is built on the same principle. Each command is like a calculator button. Press - get result. Without complex explanations, without extra words.

The structure is simple:

Command → What it does → How to use → Result

For example:

"Explain" → Reveals essence → "Explain photosynthesis" → Simple explanation

"Compare" → Shows difference → "Compare cats and dogs" → Clear comparison

"Create" → Generates new → "Create robot name" → Original name

Each command works as a separate tool. Hammer drives nails, screwdriver turns screws. Simple, clear, effective.

Don't look for complex formulas here. Look for what works. Like multiplication table - learn once, use for life.

All commands tested by thousands of users. Like folk recipes - only what really helps remains.

Use this reference like a cookbook. Don't read cover to cover - open where needed now.

And remember: the best command is one you don't need to look up in reference. It just comes naturally, like the right word in conversation.

1. BASIC COMMANDS

EXPLAIN

Action: Reveals concept essence

Format: "Explain [concept]"

Example: "Explain photosynthesis"

Modifiers:

- simply

- in detail

- step by step

- with examples

- for [target audience]

DESCRIBE

Action: Creates detailed description

Format: "Describe [object/phenomenon]"

Example: "Describe thunderstorm"

Modifiers:

- briefly
- in detail
- figuratively
- technically
- focusing on [aspect]

COMPARE

Action: Conducts comparative analysis

Format: "Compare [A] and [B]"

Example: "Compare cats and dogs"

Modifiers:

- by [criterion]
- in context of [situation]
- from perspective of [aspect]
- in table form
- with conclusions

. . .

ANALYZE

Action: Performs deep analysis

Format: "Analyze [subject]"

Example: "Analyze this text"

Modifiers:

- structure
- content
- style
- effectiveness
- impact

INVENT

Action: Generates new content

Format: "Invent [what to create]"

Example: "Invent a story"

Modifiers:

- in style of [style]
- on theme [theme]
- for [audience]
- considering [conditions]
- using [elements]

. . .

2. TRANSFORMATION COMMANDS

REPHRASE

Action: Changes wording

Format: "Rephrase [text]"

Example: "Rephrase this paragraph"

Modifiers:

- simpler
- more complex
- shorter
- more detailed
- formal/informal

TRANSLATE

Action: Changes style or format

Format: "Translate [text] into [format]"

Example: "Translate text into list"

Modifiers:

- to format [format]
- to style [style]
- for [audience]
- emphasizing [aspect]
- preserving [elements]

. . .

IMPROVE

Action: Optimizes content

Format: "Improve [object]"

Example: "Improve this text"

Modifiers:

- grammar

- style

- structure

- clarity

- persuasiveness

SHORTEN

Action: Reduces volume

Format: "Shorten [text]"

Example: "Shorten to three paragraphs"

Modifiers:

- to [volume]

- preserving [aspects]

- focusing on [elements]

- for [purpose]

- without losing [quality]

. . .

EXPAND

Action: Increases volume and detail

Format: "Expand [text]"

Example: "Expand description"

Modifiers:

- adding [aspects]

- including [elements]

- to [volume]

- in context of [context]

- focusing on [aspect]

3. RESEARCH COMMANDS

RESEARCH

Action: Conducts deep research

Format: "Research [topic]"

Example: "Research social media impact"

Modifiers:

- aspects

- causes

- effects

- relationships

- perspectives

. . .

FIND

Action: Searches specific information

Format: "Find [search object]"

Example: "Find contradictions"

Modifiers:

- all

- main

- hidden

- related

- similar

EVALUATE

Action: Provides assessment

Format: "Evaluate [evaluation object]"

Example: "Evaluate effectiveness"

Modifiers:

- by criteria

- in comparison

- from perspective

- quantitatively

- qualitatively

. . .

4. CREATION COMMANDS

CREATE

Action: Generates new content

Format: "Create [content type]"

Example: "Create project plan"

Modifiers:

- in format
- by template
- based on
- considering
- for purpose

DEVELOP

Action: Creates complex structures

Format: "Develop [object]"

Example: "Develop strategy"

Modifiers:

- step by step
- in detail
- with justification
- with examples
- with metrics

. . .

PLAN

Action: Creates action plan

Format: "Plan [process]"

Example: "Plan product launch"

Modifiers:

- by stages

- with deadlines

- with resources

- with risks

- with KPIs

5. OPTIMIZATION COMMANDS

OPTIMIZE

Action: Improves efficiency

Format: "Optimize [object]"

Example: "Optimize process"

Modifiers:

- for speed

- for quality

- for scale

- by cost

- by efficiency

STRUCTURE

Action: Organizes information

Format: "Structure [data]"

Example: "Structure report"

Modifiers:

- by topics
- by importance
- chronologically
- logically
- hierarchically

SYSTEMATIZE

Action: Creates system

Format: "Systematize [information]"

Example: "Systematize data"

Modifiers:

- by categories
- by connections
- by levels
- by functions
- by priorities

. . .

6. VERIFICATION COMMANDS

CHECK

Action: Performs verification

Format: "Check [object]"

Example: "Check text"

Modifiers:

- for errors
- for compliance
- for completeness
- for accuracy
- for relevance

VALIDATE

Action: Confirms correctness

Format: "Validate [object]"

Example: "Validate data"

Modifiers:

- by criteria
- by standards
- by requirements
- by rules

- by methodology

TEST

Action: Conducts testing

Format: "Test [object]"

Example: "Test solution"

Modifiers:

- for strength

- for flexibility

- for scalability

- for stability

- for performance

7. INTERACTION COMMANDS

DISCUSS

Action: Conducts dialogue

Format: "Discuss [topic]"

Example: "Discuss advantages and disadvantages"

Modifiers:

- in detail

- critically

- constructively

- comprehensively
- objectively

SUGGEST

Action: Generates suggestions

Format: "Suggest [what's needed]"

Example: "Suggest solution"

Modifiers:

- variants
- alternatives
- improvements
- innovations
- optimizations

ADVISE

Action: Gives recommendations

Format: "Advise [what's needed]"

Example: "Advise approach"

Modifiers:

- optimal
- practical
- effective
- accessible

- innovative

8. DEVELOPMENT COMMANDS

DEVELOP

Action: Expands idea

Format: "Develop [idea]"

Example: "Develop concept"

Modifiers:

- in detail
- creatively
- practically
- theoretically
- strategically

DEEPEN

Action: Adds depth

Format: "Deepen [aspect]"

Example: "Deepen analysis"

Modifiers:

- theoretically
- practically
- methodologically

- conceptually
- philosophically

STRENGTHEN

Action: Enhances effect

Format: "Strengthen [element]"

Example: "Strengthen argumentation"

Modifiers:

- emotionally
- logically
- factually
- stylistically
- structurally

9. SYNTHESIS COMMANDS

COMBINE

Action: Connects elements

Format: "Combine [elements]"

Example: "Combine concepts"

Modifiers:

- logically
- thematically

- functionally

- structurally

- organically

SYNTHESIZE

Action: Creates new whole

Format: "Synthesize [elements]"

Example: "Synthesize approach"

Modifiers:

- creatively

- methodically

- systematically

- innovatively

- practically

INTEGRATE

Action: Embeds elements

Format: "Integrate [what] into [where]"

Example: "Integrate solution"

Modifiers:

- smoothly

- effectively

- organically

- systematically

- optimally

10. VISUALIZATION COMMANDS

VISUALIZE

Action: Creates visual representation

Format: "Visualize [data/concept]"

Example: "Visualize process"

Modifiers:

- schematically
- in detail
- step by step
- structurally
- interactively

IMAGINE

Action: Creates figurative description

Format: "Imagine [object/situation]"

Example: "Imagine future"

Modifiers:

- figuratively
- in detail

- realistically

- creatively

- systematically

MODEL

Action: Creates model

Format: "Model [process/system]"

Example: "Model scenario"

Modifiers:

- mathematically

- conceptually

- visually

- dynamically

- interactively

APPENDIX B: PROMPT TEMPLATES

You know how they teach swimming? Not with hydrodynamics theory. They start with basics: hold the edge, kick your legs, breathe.

This template collection works the same way. No complex theory - just proven patterns that will help you "stay afloat" in the ocean of prompts.

Each template is like a life preserver. Take it, use it, swim on. When you lcarn - you'll crcatc your own.

Templates are collected on the "simple to complex" principle. Like a swimming textbook: first we hold the edge, then we dog paddle, then we master the crawl.

Don't try to memorize everything at once. Start with one template, master it, move to the next. Like in sports - first basic movements, then complex combinations.

Each template is proven by practice. Like folk tales - only those that survived centuries remain, because they work.

Use these templates as building blocks. First following instructions, then creating your own constructions.

And remember: the best template is one you've made your own. Like a favorite sweater - uncomfortable at first, then you don't want to take it off.

GENERAL TEMPLATES

1. CONCEPT EXPLANATION

"Explain [concept] in simple terms, as if explaining to [target audience]. Use understandable examples from everyday life. Break the explanation into [number] key points. End with a brief one-sentence summary."

2. STEP-BY-STEP INSTRUCTION

"Create a step-by-step instruction for [action]. Start with required materials/tools. Break the process into clear, numbered steps. For each step, indicate approximate completion time. Add safety tips and possible mistakes. Conclude with frequently asked questions and answers."

. . .

3. COMPARATIVE ANALYSIS

"Compare [A] and [B] using the following criteria:

1. [criterion 1]

2. [criterion 2]

3. [criterion 3]

...

For each criterion, indicate advantages and disadvantages of both options. End with general conclusion and recommendation."

4. IDEA GENERATION

"Create a list of [number] original ideas for [task]. Each idea should be:

- Realistic

- Feasible within [constraints]

- Unique

For each idea indicate:

1. Brief description

2. Main advantages

3. Possible challenges

4. Approximate resources for implementation"

5. PROBLEM ANALYSIS

"Analyze the problem [problem] using the following structure:

1. Situation description

2. Root causes

3. Impact on [stakeholders]

4. Existing solutions

5. Proposed alternatives

6. Success criteria

7. Action plan

8. Result evaluation metrics"

CREATIVE TEMPLATES

STORY CREATION

"Create a story with the following parameters:

Genre: [genre]

Length: [volume]

Main character: [description]

Setting: [place and time]

Main conflict: [conflict]

Theme: [theme]

Special requirements:

- [requirement 1]

- [requirement 2]

Structure:

1. Setup

2. Development

3. Climax

4. Resolution"

CHARACTER GENERATION

"Create a detailed character profile:

1. Basic information

- Name:

- Age:

- Appearance:

2. Background

- Origin:

- Key events:

- Traumas/achievements:

3. Personality

- Main traits:

- Motivation:

- Fears:

- Dreams:

4. Relationships

- Family:

- Friends:

- Enemies:

5. Skills and abilities

6. Role in story"

DIALOGUE CREATION

"Create a dialogue between [character 1] and [character 2] about [topic].

Conditions:

- Length: [number] of exchanges

- Emotional tone: [tone]

- Dialogue goal: [goal]

- Subtext: [subtext]

Character features:

[Character 1]: [characteristics]

[Character 2]: [characteristics]"

SCENE DESCRIPTION

"Create a detailed scene description:

Location: [location]

Time: [time of day/year]

Atmosphere: [mood]

Include description of:

1. Visual details

2. Sounds

3. Smells

4. Tactile sensations

5. Movement

6. Lighting

Special focus on: [element]"

ANALYTICAL TEMPLATES

SWOT ANALYSIS

"Conduct SWOT analysis for [analysis object]:

Strengths:

- [point 1]
- [point 2]

Weaknesses:

- [point 1]
- [point 2]

Opportunities:

- [point 1]
- [point 2]

Threats:

- [point 1]
- [point 2]

For each point indicate:

1. Impact level

2. Probability

3. Possible actions"

TREND ANALYSIS

"Analyze trends in [area] using following parameters:

1. Current state

2. Historical context

3. Key change drivers

4. Main trends:

- Short-term (1-2 years)

- Medium-term (3-5 years)

- Long-term (5+ years)

5. Impact on:

- [aspect 1]

- [aspect 2]

6. Recommendations"

RISK ASSESSMENT

"Conduct risk assessment for [project/situation]:

For each risk indicate:

1. Description

2. Probability (1-5)

3. Impact (1-5)

4. Overall rating (Probability × Impact)

5. Triggers

6. Preventive measures

7. Response plan

8. Responsible persons

9. Monitoring"

TECHNICAL TEMPLATES

API DOCUMENTATION

"Create documentation for API endpoint:

Endpoint: [URL]

Method: [GET/POST/PUT/DELETE]

Description: [functionality description]

Request parameters:

- [parameter 1]: [type] - [description]

- [parameter 2]: [type] - [description]

Headers:

- [header 1]: [value]

Request body:

```json

[request body example]
```

```

Response:

```json

[response example]

```

Response codes:

- 200: [description]

- 400: [description]

- 500: [description]

Usage examples:

[example 1]

[example 2]"

TECHNICAL SPECIFICATION

"Create technical specification for [product/system]:

1. Overview

- Purpose

- Scope

- Target audience

2. Functional requirements

- [requirement 1]

- [requirement 2]

3. Non-functional requirements
```

- Performance

- Security

- Scalability

4. Architecture

- Components

- Interactions

- Interfaces

5. Technology stack

6. Constraints

7. Dependencies

8. Implementation plan"

TEST REPORT

"Create test report for [system/functionality]:

1. General information

- Test date

- Version

- Environment

2. Test scope

- What was tested

- What wasn't included

3. Test types conducted

- [test type 1]

- [test type 2]

4. Results

- Tests passed: [number]

- Bugs found: [number]

5. Issues discovered

- Critical: [list]

- Major: [list]

- Minor: [list]

6. Recommendations

7. Conclusion"

BUSINESS TEMPLATES

BUSINESS PLAN

"Create brief business plan for [project]:

1. Executive summary

2. Product/service description

- Unique value proposition

- Target audience

- Problem solved

3. Market analysis

- Market size

- Competitors

- Advantages

4. Marketing strategy

5. Operations plan

6. Financial plan

- Initial investment

- Revenue forecast

- Expense forecast

- Break-even point

7. Risks and opportunities

8. Implementation plan"

MARKETING STRATEGY

"Develop marketing strategy for [product/service]:

1. Market analysis

- Target audience

- Competitors

- Trends

2. Positioning

- USP

- Key messages

3. Promotion channels

- [channel 1]

- [channel 2]

4. Content strategy

5. Budget

6. KPIs

7. Implementation schedule

8. Effectiveness evaluation methods"

COMPETITOR ANALYSIS

"Conduct competitor analysis for [company/product]:

1. Main competitors

For each competitor:

- General information

- Products/services

- Target audience

- Pricing policy

- Sales channels

- Marketing strategy

- Strengths

- Weaknesses

2. Comparative analysis

3. Market shares

4. Unique advantages

5. Differentiation opportunities

6. Recommendations"

. . .

EDUCATIONAL TEMPLATES

CURRICULUM

"Create curriculum for topic [topic]:

1. Learning objectives

2. Target audience

3. Prerequisites

4. Course structure:

Module 1: [name]

- Topics

- Practical assignments

- Study time

[repeat for each module]

5. Teaching methods

6. Materials

7. Results assessment

8. Additional resources"

LEARNING MATERIAL

"Create learning material for topic [topic]:

1. Introduction

- Relevance

- Lesson objectives

2. Main part

- Concept 1

* Explanation

* Examples

* Practice

[repeat for each concept]

3. Practical assignments

4. Self-check questions

5. Additional materials

6. Glossary

7. Sources"

KNOWLEDGE ASSESSMENT

"Create assessment materials for topic [topic]:

1. Test questions

- Single correct answer

- Multiple choice

- Matching

2. Practical tasks

3. Case studies

4. Project assignments

5. Assessment criteria

6. Rubrics

7. Feedback methods"

RESEARCH TEMPLATES

RESEARCH PLAN

"Create research plan [topic]:

1. Introduction

- Relevance

- Research goal

- Tasks

- Hypotheses

2. Methodology

Data collection methods

- Analysis methods

- Sample

3. Research stages

4. Resources

5. Expected results

6. Limitations

7. Work schedule

8. Budget"

. . .

LITERATURE REVIEW

"Conduct literature review on topic [topic]:

1. Sources overview

For each source:

- Full description

- Main ideas

- Methodology

- Results

- Limitations

2. Information synthesis

3. Identified gaps

4. Contradictions

5. Trends

6. Conclusions"

RESEARCH REPORT

"Create research report on topic [topic]:

1. Abstract

2. Introduction

- Relevance

- Goals and objectives

- Hypotheses

3. Methodology

4. Results

5. Discussion

6. Conclusions

7. Recommendations

8. References

9. Appendices"

8. CONTENT TEMPLATES

ARTICLE

"Create article on topic [topic]:

1. Headline

- Main

- Subheading

2. Introduction

- Hook

- Context

- Thesis

3. Main body

- Key point 1

* Evidence

* Examples

[repeat for each point]

4. Conclusion

5. Call to action"

PRESS RELEASE

"Create press release about [event/announcement]:

1. Headline

2. Subheading

3. Location and date

4. Lead paragraph

5. Main text

- Quote 1

- Context

- Quote 2

6. Background information

7. Contacts

8. Notes for editors"

PRODUCT DESCRIPTION

"Create product description [product]:

1. Brief description

2. Key features

3. Benefits

4. Technical specifications

5. Use cases

6. Target audience

7. Comparison with alternatives

8. Price and availability

9. Warranty and support"

SPECIALIZED TEMPLATES

REVIEW

"Create review of [object]:

1. General information

2. First impression

3. Detailed analysis

- [aspect 1]

- [aspect 2]

4. Strengths

5. Weaknesses

6. Comparison with alternatives

7. Target audience

8. Rating

9. Conclusion"

USER MANUAL

"Create user manual for [product]:

1. Introduction

2. Getting started

- Installation

- Setup

3. Main functions

For each function:

- Description

- Step-by-step instruction

- Screenshots

- Tips

4. Troubleshooting

5. FAQ

6. Glossary

7. Technical support"

EXPERIMENT PROTOCOL

"Create experiment protocol [name]:

1. Experiment goal

2. Materials and equipment

3. Methodology

- Preparation

- Procedure

- Measurements

4. Safety

5. Data collection

6. Results analysis

7. Conclusions

8. Recommendations"

INTERACTIVE TEMPLATES

DIALOGUE SCENARIO

"Create dialogue interaction scenario for [situation]:

1. Initial greeting

2. Need identification

3. Responses to typical questions

4. Scripts for difficult situations

5. Conversation closing

For each stage:

- System replies

- Expected user responses

- Alternative paths"

INTERACTIVE STORY

"Create interactive story with [theme]:

1. Initial situation

2. Key choice points

For each point:

- Situation description

- Choice options

- Consequences of each choice

3. Possible endings

4. Hidden paths

5. Achievements"

APPENDIX C: CHECKLISTS

You know how an airplane takes off? The pilot checks each system from a list. They don't rely on memory - they use a proven checklist.

These checklists work the same way. No magic - just a clear sequence of checks that ensures the safe "takeoff" of your prompt.

Each list is like pre-flight preparation. Complete all items - you can take off. Miss something - better check again.

The lists are compiled on the "necessary and sufficient" principle. Like a first aid kit - everything needed is there, nothing superfluous.

Don't try to keep everything in your head. Use lists as external memory. Like a knot on a handkerchief - a simple reminder of what's important.

Each list is proven by practice. Like safety rules - written in the blood of mistakes and failures.

Use these lists as insurance. At first it seems unnecessary, then you realize - this is what saved you from mistakes.

And remember: the best list is the one you actually use. Like a toothbrush - it doesn't matter how smart it is, what matters is that you use it every day.

1. BASIC PROMPT CHECK

□ Purpose

- Main task clearly defined

- Desired result understood

- Success criteria specified

□ Structure

- Logical sequence

- Clear separation of parts

- Coherence of elements

□ Language

- Unambiguous wording

- No jargon

- Correct punctuation

□ Context

- Necessary background

- Important limitations

- Key parameters

□ Format

- Compliance with system requirements

- Optimal length

- Proper formatting

2. EFFECTIVENESS CHECK

□ Clarity

- Task understandable at first reading

- No ambiguities

- All terms defined

□ Specificity

- Precise parameters

- Measurable criteria

- Clear boundaries

□ Relevance

- All parts relate to task

- No excess information

- Focus on goal

□ Completeness

- All necessary details included

- No missing steps

- Sufficient context

□ Feasibility

- Realistic requirements

- Achievable goals

- Available resources

. . .

3. SAFETY CHECK

□ Ethics

- Compliance with ethical norms

- No bias

- Respect for users

□ Confidentiality

- Personal data protection

- Information security

- Privacy maintenance

□ Limitations

- Prohibited content check

- Platform rules compliance

- Age restrictions consideration

□ Validation

- Source verification

- Fact checking

- Statement confirmation

□ Security

- No malicious code

- Injection protection

- Abuse prevention

. . .

4. OPTIMIZATION CHECK

□ Efficiency

- Minimal redundancy

- Optimal token use

- Effective structure

□ Scalability

- Expansion possibility

- Adaptability to changes

- Setting flexibility

□ Performance

- Quick execution

- Resource economy

- Optimal load

□ Reliability

- Error resistance

- Result predictability

- Operation stability

□ Maintainability

- Easy updating

- Simple modification

- Clear structure

5. USER EXPERIENCE CHECK

□ Accessibility

- Understandable for target audience

- Easy to use

- Clear instructions

□ Convenience

- Logical structure

- Intuitive navigation

- Convenient format

□ Feedback

- Clear messages

- Informative responses

- Useful hints

□ Flexibility

- Adaptability to different scenarios

- User error resilience

- Adjustment possibility

□ Effectiveness

- Quick goal achievement

- Minimum necessary actions

- Optimal solution path

6. INTEGRATION CHECK

□ Compatibility

- Works with different systems

- Meets standards

- Universal format

□ Interaction

- Correct data transfer

- Proper response handling

- Reliable connections

□ Synchronization

- Action coordination

- Correct sequence

- No conflicts

□ Scaling

- Expansion possibility

- Growth support

- Load adaptability

□ Monitoring

- Status tracking

- Execution control

- Result analysis

7. DOCUMENTATION CHECK

□ Completeness

- All aspects described

- Sufficient details

- All scenarios covered

□ Accuracy

- Information correctness

- Data relevance

- Description accuracy

□ Clarity

- Clear presentation

- Logical structure

- Accessible explanations

□ Practicality

- Useful examples

- Practical advice

- Real scenarios

□ Support

- Contact for questions

- Problem-solving instructions

- Help resources

8. TESTING CHECK

□ Functionality

- All functions work

- Correct results

- Proper processing

□ Reliability

- Stable operation

- Error resilience

- Predictable behavior

□ Performance

- Quick response

- Efficient resource use

- Optimal load

□ Security

- Data protection

- Vulnerability prevention

- Access control

□ Compatibility

- Works in different conditions

- Supports different platforms

- System integration

9. UPDATE CHECK

□ Relevance

- Meets current requirements

- Uses latest versions

- Considers new capabilities

□ Compatibility

- Works with new versions

- Supports old functions

- Backward compatibility

□ Improvements

- New features

- Operation optimization

- Bug fixes

□ Documentation

- Description updates

- Example updates

- New instructions

□ Testing

- New function testing

- Regression testing

- Change validation

10. FINAL CHECK

□ Overall Assessment

- Goal achievement

- Requirement compliance

- Result quality

□ Efficiency

- Solution optimality
- Resource use rationality
- Operation speed

□ Reliability

- Operation stability
- Error resilience
- Result predictability

□ Convenience

- Easy to use
- Clear operation
- Function accessibility

□ Readiness

- Implementation completeness
- All aspects finished
- Ready for use

ADDITIONAL LISTS

11. CREATIVITY CHECK

□ Originality

- Approach uniqueness
- Solution novelty
- Creative element

□ Flexibility

- Adaptability to different tasks

- Modification possibility

- Application variety

□ Development

- Improvement potential

- Expansion possibilities

- Development prospects

□ Innovation

- New approach use

- Advanced method application

- Experimental elements

□ Balance

- Tradition and innovation combination

- Form and content balance

- Element harmony

12. ETHICS AND VALUES CHECK

□ Ethical Principles

- Moral norm compliance

- User respect

- Approach honesty

□ Social Responsibility

- Society benefit

- Solution sustainability

- Sustainable development

□ Inclusivity

- Accessibility for all

- Different needs consideration

- No discrimination

□ Transparency

- Process openness

- Decision clarity

- Information accessibility

□ Responsibility

- Consequence consideration

- Feedback readiness

- Responsibility acceptance

APPENDIX D: GLOSSARY

Remember your first conversation in a foreign language? Each word - a discovery. Each phrase - a victory. Each understood meaning - joy.

This glossary is your phrasebook in the world of prompts. Not a dry dictionary of terms, but a living bridge between familiar words and new meanings.

Each definition is like a translation from one language to another.

Complex things in simple words. Without scientific jargon, without unnecessary complications.

Terms are collected on the "need now" principle. Like a travel phrasebook - everything that might be useful, nothing superfluous.

Don't try to learn everything at once. Master terms in work, when they're really needed. Like foreign words - they're better remembered when used in practice.

Each term is proven by practice. Like living language - only words that are actually used remain.

Use this glossary as a map of new territory. At first everything seems foreign, then becomes familiar.

And remember: the best term is one you can explain to another. Like native language - it's not important how many words you know, what matters is how clearly you can express thought.

2

PROMPT ENGINEERING GLOSSARY

A

Agent - Role or personality assumed by AI in dialogue. For example, "Act as an experienced editor."

Adaptive prompt - A prompt that changes depending on context or previous responses.

Token analysis - Evaluation of quantity and efficiency of token use in a prompt.

Archetypal prompt - Basic prompt template serving as foundation for variations.

Atomic prompt - Simplest, indivisible prompt performing one specific function.

B

Base context - Minimum information necessary for correct prompt interpretation.

Prompt balancing - Optimization of relationship between various prompt elements.

Understanding barrier - Obstacle in communication between human and AI.

Prompt safety - Measures to prevent unwanted or dangerous results.

Prompt bifurcation - Branching of prompt into alternative development paths.

C

Context - Information environment determining prompt interpretation.

Chain of thought - Sequence of logical steps in prompt.

Coherence - Logical connectivity and consistency of prompt.

Context window - Amount of information available to AI for analysis.

Complexity - Level of intricacy in prompt structure and logic.

D

Dynamic prompt - Prompt changing during dialogue.

Depth - Level of detail and complexity in prompt.

Decomposition - Breaking complex task into simple prompts.

Drift - Gradual deviation from original context in long dialogues.

Direction - Main aim or goal of prompt.

E

Efficiency - Ratio of result to resources used.

Elasticity - Prompt's ability to stretch and compress.

Emergence - Appearance of new properties in prompt interactions.

Enhancement - Techniques for improving prompt effectiveness.

Explicit context - Clearly stated contextual information.

F

Feedback - Information about prompt operation results.

Filtering - Screening out irrelevant information.

Flow - Smooth progression of prompt elements.

Formalization - Bringing prompt to standard form.

Framework - Structure supporting prompt operation.

G

Generative prompt - Prompt aimed at creating new content.

Granularity - Degree of detail in prompt.

Growth - Prompt's ability to develop and improve.

Guidance - Direction provided by prompt.

Guard rails - Protective limitations in prompt.

H

Hierarchy - System of prompt subordination.

Holistic approach - Considering prompt as complete system.

Heuristics - Practical rules for creating prompts.

Harmony - Balance between prompt elements.

Hook - Element capturing attention in prompt.

I

Idempotency - Property of prompt giving same result when reapplied.

Implementation - Practical application of prompt.

Injection - Adding additional contextual information.

Integration - Combining prompts with other systems.

Intelligence - Level of prompt's adaptive capability.

J

Jailbreak - Attempt to bypass prompt restrictions.

Junction - Point where different prompt paths meet.

Journey - User's path through prompt interaction.

Judgment - Evaluation capability in prompt.

Justification - Reasoning behind prompt decisions.

K

Knowledge base - Information foundation for prompt.

Kernel - Core element of prompt.

Key - Essential element unlocking prompt functionality.

Kinetics - Dynamic behavior of prompt.

Knowledge graph - Network of prompt-related information.

L

Layer - Level of prompt organization.

Learning - Prompt's ability to improve from experience.

Legacy - Long-term impact of prompt.

Leverage - Using prompt capabilities effectively.

Logic - Reasoning structure in prompt.

M

Mapping - Creating connections between prompt elements.

Memory - Information retention in prompt system.

Metadata - Additional information about prompt.

Migration - Moving prompt between systems.

Modulation - Adjusting prompt parameters.

N

Navigation - Moving through prompt structure.

Nested prompt - Prompt containing other prompts.

Network - Interconnected system of prompts.

Neutrality - Lack of bias in prompt formulation.

Node - Connection point in prompt structure.

. . .

O

Objective - Goal of prompt operation.

Optimization - Improving prompt effectiveness.

Orchestra - Coordinated prompt system.

Output - Result of prompt operation.

Override - Changing default prompt behavior.

P

Pattern - Repeating prompt structure.

Performance - Prompt operation effectiveness.

Persistence - Context maintenance between sessions.

Pipeline - Sequence of prompt operations.

Plasticity - Prompt's ability to adapt.

Q

Quality - Overall prompt effectiveness.

Query - Specific prompt request.

Quantum prompt - Prompt working with multiple possible states.

Queue - Sequence of waiting prompts.

Quotient - Measure of prompt effectiveness.

R

Recursion - Prompt referring to itself.

Refinement - Improving prompt quality.

Reliability - Consistency of prompt operation.

Resilience - Ability to maintain effectiveness despite changes.

Response - System's answer to prompt.

S

Safety - Protection against unwanted results.

Scaling - Adapting prompt to different sizes.

Scope - Range of prompt application.

Sequence - Order of prompt elements.

Structure - Organization of prompt elements.

T

Template - Basic structure for creating prompts.

Testing - Verifying prompt effectiveness.

Threshold - Point of significant change in prompt behavior.

Training - Preparing prompt for operation.

Transformation - Change in prompt state.

U

Understanding - Comprehension of prompt purpose.

Unity - Coherence of prompt elements.

Universal - Applicable to various situations.

Upgrade - Improving prompt capabilities.

Utility - Practical usefulness of prompt.

V

Validation - Confirming prompt correctness.

Value - Worth of prompt operation.

Vector - Direction of prompt development.

Version - Specific prompt iteration.

Visibility - Clarity of prompt operation.

W

Workflow - Sequence of prompt operations.

Wrapper - External prompt structure.

Weight - Importance of prompt elements.

Width - Breadth of prompt application.

Wisdom - Accumulated prompt knowledge.

X

X-factor - Unique prompt characteristic.

XML - Structured prompt format.

Cross-reference - Connection between prompts.

Exchange - Information flow between prompts.

Extension - Additional prompt capability.

Y

Yield - Productive output of prompt.

Yoke - Connection between prompt elements.

Yesterday - Historical prompt data.

Yearning - Desired prompt state.

Youth - Early prompt development stage.

Z

Zero-shot - Prompt working without training.

Zenith - Peak prompt performance.

Zone - Area of prompt operation.

Zoom - Focus on specific prompt aspect.

Zest - Energy in prompt operation.

This glossary continues to evolve as the field of prompt engineering develops. Like a living language, it grows and changes with practice and discovery. Use it not as a final authority, but as a starting point for your own understanding and development in the art of prompt engineering.

3

FROM AUTHOR

Dear Reader,

I created this book using MUDRIA.AI - a quantum-simulated system that I developed to enhance human capabilities. This is not just an artificial intelligence system, but a quantum amplifier of human potential in all spheres, including creativity.

Many authors already use AI in their work without advertising this fact. Why am I openly talking about using AI? Because I believe the future lies in honest and open collaboration between humans and technology. MUDRIA.AI doesn't replace the author but helps create deeper, more useful, and more inspiring works.

Every word in this book has primarily passed through my heart and mind but was enhanced by MUDRIA.AI's quantum algorithms. This allowed us to achieve a level of depth and practical value that would have been impossible otherwise.

You might notice that the text seems unusually crystal clear, and the emotions remarkably precise. Some might find this "too perfect."

But remember: once, people thought photographs, recorded music, and cinema seemed unnatural... Today, they're an integral part of our lives. Technology didn't kill painting, live music, or theater - it made art more accessible and diverse.

The same is happening now with literature. MUDRIA.AI doesn't threaten human creativity - it makes it more accessible, profound, and refined. It's a new tool, just as the printing press once opened a new era in the spread of knowledge.

Distinguishing text created with MUDRIA.AI from one written by a human alone is indeed challenging. But it's not because the system "imitates" humans. It amplifies the author's natural abilities, helping express thoughts and feelings with maximum clarity and power. It's as if an artist discovered new, incredible colors, allowing them to convey what previously seemed inexpressible.

I believe in openness and accessibility of knowledge. Therefore, all my books created with MUDRIA.AI are distributed electronically for free. By purchasing the print version, you're supporting the project's development, helping make human potential enhancement technologies available to everyone.

We stand on the threshold of a new era of creativity, where technology doesn't replace humans but unleashes their limitless potential. This book is a small step in this exciting journey into the future we're creating together.

Welcome to the new era of creativity!

With respect,

Oleh Konko

ABOUT THE AUTHOR

Oleh Konko works at the intersection of consciousness studies, technology, and human potential. Through his books, he makes transformative knowledge accessible to everyone, bridging science and wisdom to illuminate paths toward human flourishing.

FREE DISTRIBUTION NOTICE

SUPPORT THE PROJECT

If you find this book valuable, consider supporting the project at website: mudria.ai

Physical copies available through major retailers and mudria.ai

Reproducibility Notice: All theoretical frameworks, mathematical proofs, and computational methods described in this work are designed to be independently reproducible. Source code and additional materials are available at mudria.ai

Version Control:

Print Edition: 1.00

Digital Edition: 1.00

www.ingramcontent.com/pod-product-compliance
Lightning Source LLC
LaVergne TN
LVHW100327210926
848480LV00003B/1281
* 9 7 9 8 2 3 0 8 0 0 7 5 0 *